60 Days to Paradise

We want a new world!
We want Paradise!

By Dr. Edward Schellhammer

3rd Edition 2014, revised.
© Copyright. Dr. Edward Schellhammer.
All Rights Reserved.

ISBN-13: 978-1480177369
ISBN-10: 1480177369

www.EdwardSchellhammer.com

Table of Contents

We want a new world!
We want Paradise!

We want to live with a holistic positive life philosophy with real hope.
We want to understand our feelings and to be able to manage them.
We want to live love, our genuine psychical needs, with truthfulness.
We want to see through, to think profoundly and also in creative ways.
We want to understand ourselves, our inner life, and our behavior.
We want to acquire knowledge and skills to efficiently master life.
We want to become an authentic, fully self-realized and strong person.
We want to have real, efficient, constructive ideals, values, norms, and rules.
We want to live a new, authentic life style with an excellent self-management.
We want to prepare ourselves for a happy relationship and family life.
We want to live our desire for sex and tenderness with a lot of love.
We want to live free from biographical burdens and unconscious complexes.
We want to be able to solve difficulties, crises, problems, and conflicts.
We want to praise and to live the deepest eternal meaning of marriage.
We want to succeed with our children by making them authentic and strong.
We want to live and grow with a genuine meaning of life, rooted inside.
We want to understand our dreams – the messages from the inner Spirit.
We want to correctly meditate and practice mental training for wellness.
We want to live all Archetypes of the Soul for our complete fulfillment.
We want to care for our health, for the environment, humanity, and the planet.
We want peace, a global balance of power, a fair distribution of resources.
We want all politicians, CEOs, and rulers to be rooted in the inner Spirit.
We want the media to inform us about what is really important on this earth.
We want freedom of speech and thought as well as transparency in political life.
We want a new education that respects and promotes the inner life and the truth.

As long as you reject the Paradise,
you are also on the dark side of humanity.

We don't want hell on earth!

We don't want superficiality, lies, life lies, cheat, falseness, bigotry, rigidity, narcissism, stubbornness, big mouths, arrogance, ignorance, unreasonableness, sadism, disrespect, stone-cold coolness and scrupulousness.

We don't want people that poison humanity with their immorality, blown up ego, megalomania, perversion, dogmatism and fundamentalism, superstition, lunacy, madness, extreme greed, evil purposes, and religious psychosis.

We don't want to be deceived, lured, brainwashed and manipulated, oppressed and led into sick meanders, exploited as a human and financially abused like slaves, and treated as vacuous soulless humans to make a few selected individuals into super-billionaires.

We don't want pollution, contamination, climate change, environmental destruction, exploitation of resources, speculations, global poverty and misery, injustice, nuclear waste, armament, wars, fascism, and the new Nazi-like laws and practices.

We don't want façades or masks that hide or distort realities; we don't want to be the puppets of politicians and the economy or the industry, and we don't want to be detracted from the truth and misled with false promises.

**Stand and fight for the Paradise
or you belong to hell on earth.**

WHAT DO YOU WANT? DECIDE NOW!

"**60 Days to Paradise**" will provide you with all the knowledge and skills you need to solve problems, become successful, find happiness and achieve a genuine fulfillment. Read one article per day and apply the practical tips and suggestions to change your life for the better!

Every single day you will become stronger, more confident and you will reach a new quality level in your personal life. Extend your knowledge, acquire new skills and apply them to efficiently master your life, grow with your inner life and get your ticket to Paradise!

The solution for humanity and the earth has a clear and feasible perspective: If 500 million people live the **60 Days to Paradise**, humanity and the earth will have the best possible path towards a good future.

1. Build up a Positive Life Philosophy

👍 *You need an all-sided balanced concept of a positive life philosophy.*

👍 *A positive life philosophy includes the entire psychical-spiritual organism.*

👍 *The long-term and lateral effects of your behavior form part of a positive life philosophy.*

👍 *A positive life philosophy includes forming your efficient skills to master life.*

👍 *The global state of humanity and the earth are always taken into consideration in a positive life philosophy.*

👍 *Money, job, work, business, corporate groups, and politics must fulfill humans and allow everyone a fair life.*

The network of a Positive Life Philosophy includes:

- Openness to learn and readiness for change.
- Flexible integration of life realities.
- Living with social skills and life techniques.
- Being responsible for your health and for the environment.
- Forming an efficient self-management.
- Liberation from the archaic generation-destiny.

- Establishing a harmony between the inner and external life.

- Giving the inner life and human values the highest priority.

- Consciousness about the inner world and the external realities.

- Understanding humanity as a community on a spiritual path.

- Solidarity with the human community in all basic human needs.

- Self-control within the inner and external world.

- Cleaning the subconscious to achieve inner peace and peace on earth.

- Dissolution and balance of all contradictory inner forces.

- Knowledge about the complexity of the inner and external life.

- Many-sided consciousness about mankind and the world.

- Differentiated perception of one's own reality.

- Living consciously with Spirit and love for humanity.

 Either you live in the truth or you live lies. There is definitely no paradise for those who do not search for the truth and live it! You decide!

2. Cherish, Live and Protect Human Values

✋ *All human values must be founded in the psychical-spiritual organism.*

✋ *All human values express evolutionary and archetypal potentials.*

✋ *All human values are embedded in the social and natural environment.*

✋ *All human values must be considered in the network of humanity as a unity.*

✋ *Humanity's future lies in the Archetypes of the Soul and the human values.*

The absolute unconditional human values:

➜ All single psychical and spiritual functions express human values.

➜ The psychical-spiritual organism is itself a precious human value.

➜ Development of the psychical-spiritual organism is a human value.

➜ The Archetypes of the Soul are of highest eternal human value.

Forming and shaping the human values is your

responsibility:

- Love, trust, truthfulness, happiness, freedom, hope, satisfaction, fulfillment
- Authenticity, genuineness, self-realization, expansion of personality
- Self-identity, self-esteem, self-confidence, strong will, determination, firmness
- Moral character, integrity, balanced personality, self-control, talents
- Fun, pleasure, joy of life, wellbeing, zest for life, lust, cultural expressions
- Ability to perform, skills, creativity, self-management, personal life style
- Creating environment for humans and for the fulfillment of all humans

 Either you live human values or you live hell. There is no paradise unless you live the human values! You decide!

3. Love Being on this Earth

👍 *Value your physical being, your psychological being, your talents, your special character, and your spiritual potentials.*

👍 *Value everything life offers you to live and to realize yourself, including all the small things that can make you enjoy life.*

👍 *Value all possibilities to learn for your development, for your work, for your home, for your life with a partner, for a relationship and for a family.*

👍 *Value what your society can give you: a frame for your life, infrastructure, a cultural identity, and much more.*

👍 *Value the history of your country and culture with all the countless efforts made for a better and more comfortable life during centuries by all the pioneers.*

Love is for: yourself, your partner, your children, the world of children and adolescents, the world of adults and elderly people, humanity and the earth (nature), the inner Spirit and God.

Abilities to love are expressed in:
▪ Having an active interest in the psychical-spiritual life of humans.

- Giving high importance to one's own psychical-spiritual life.
- Consciously forming the entire psychical inner life.
- Valuing, promoting and using one's own real resources.
- Contemplating about the high values of human beings.
- Discovering spirituality inside oneself and in other people.
- Being vigilant with the destructive forces of the unconscious.
- Caring for constructive and many-sided thinking and acting.
- Being open to live one's own desires in a creative way.
- Respecting the healthy needs of the body and taking care of them.
- Regularly and actively experiencing nature and valuing it.
- Protecting and caring for the values of family and relationship.

 Either you learn to love being on this earth or you will end up in complete destructiveness. There is no paradise without love for being on this earth! You decide!

4. Create a Constant Process of Changes

👍 *You can develop yourself and grow holistically.*

👍 *You can renew yourself from your innermost being.*

👍 *You can change yourself whenever you want.*

👍 *You can change yourself and your life towards more authenticity, love, satisfaction, and happiness.*

👍 *You must want to change and to motivate yourself for improvements.*

👍 *Changing your human being and your life into the direction of more quality at the same time leads to a genuine self-fulfillment.*

You can activate hope, flexibility and initiative for changes:
- Change expectations by adapting them to realistic opportunities.
- Change your self-image by changing your self-perception.
- Realize your talents and potentials as much as possible.
- Resolve conflicts with yourself, your partner, and with life.
- Find a higher satisfaction through learning processes.
- Clarify your feelings and attitudes that hinder changes.
- Develop yourself with attitudes of honesty and truthfulness.
- Change rigid attitudes and beliefs that are inapplicable for

life.

- Become free from unconscious, inefficient and destructive coding.

- Transform egoism and narcissism through self-reflection.

- Improve yourself to become an all-sided balanced person.

- Change exaggerated ideals and illusions about yourself, life and God.

- Critically reflect the manifold content of your consciousness.

- Elaborate your biography in order to grow towards authenticity.

- Change your destructive behavior through self-reflection.

- Elaborate difficult situations in your inner and external life.

- Learning about humans and life always leads to changes.

- Constructive living with a partner always requires learning.

- Having children demands learning from your children.

 Either you create a process of changes or you end up as a brainwashed and manipulated human being. There is no paradise without changes towards authenticity and efficiency! You decide!

5. Care for Holistic Life Aims

👍 *You can only achieve high life aims if you form yourself holistically.*

👍 *You only have one life and a limited life time to realize yourself in the best possible way.*

👍 *If you don't focus on realistic life aims, including your inner life, you will end up caught in a web of lies and deceit.*

👍 *All realistic life aims serve your psychical-spiritual growth and the psychical-spiritual evolution.*

How to develop your holistic life aims:

→ Spend time on your all-inclusive and extensive <u>self-knowledge</u>.

→ Increasingly develop a more differentiated <u>self-image</u>.

→ Acquire many-sided <u>knowledge about humans</u> and the world.

→ Understand <u>transcendence</u> through psychical-spiritual growth.

→ Experience the <u>existence</u> in the complexity of the inner-external life.

→ Give importance to a strong and positive <u>self-experience</u>.

→ Become free from <u>defense mechanisms</u> and projection.

- ➜ Openly manage a dynamic <u>integration of all life realities</u>.

- ➜ Consciously form a strong <u>will</u>.

- ➜ Form your <u>self-control</u> in the complexity of the inner-external world.

- ➜ Completely elaborate your <u>unconscious life</u>.

- ➜ Build up a differentiated <u>perception</u> of all realities.

- ➜ Operate with a creative and constructive <u>thinking</u> by using clear words.

- ➜ Be open to <u>learn</u> and gradually change and extend.

- ➜ Satisfy your genuine <u>inner needs</u> in a balanced way.

- ➜ Balance your many-sided <u>emotional life</u>.

- ➜ Make your ability to <u>love</u> sustainable and operational.

- ➜ Form a flexible and vital <u>psychodynamic</u>.

- ➜ Foster your communication with the <u>inner Spirit</u> (dreams).

- ➜ Act consciously in relation to the entire <u>psychical organism</u>.

- ➜ <u>Develop</u> yourself with love and the inner Spirit.

- ➜ Live and become a vivid copy of the Archetype of <u>fulfillment</u>.

 Either you make an effort to live realistic life aims or you will end up in a complete chaos of evil influences and dark meanders. There is no paradise for people without realistic life aims! You decide!

6. Become a Human Being

👍 *The most essential meaning of life is to become an evolutionary human being.*

👍 *A human being is determined by the inner psychical-spiritual life, founded in the Archetypes of the Soul.*

👍 *The core characteristics of an "evolutionary human being" include the inner life as well as the external life.*

Practical orientations:

- Accept the entire psychical life and consciously form all psychical forces.
- Liberate yourself from the inner burdens of your biography.
- Free yourself from your unconscious projections.
- Constructively elaborate the images in your unconscious and progressively promote life.
- Continuously find inner orientation through dream interpretation, meditation and contemplation.
- Integrate and elaborate all the uncomfortable, weak and different "things" in life.
- Relationships and social interactions must respect the psychical-spiritual development.
- Politics and the economy must be at the service of the

psychical-spiritual development of humanity

- Deal with nature, the world of animals, and the environment with love and respect for the inner Spirit.
- Promote a differentiated development and use the power of love and the inner Spirit.
- Develop flexibility and inner freedom towards material goods and external values.
- Give effort for psychical-spiritual performances, characterized by love and Spirit as highest values.

→ You must become open to acquiring knowledge and to learning.

→ You must become aware of your inner and external life.

→ You must be all-sided balanced in your inner and external life.

→ You must efficiently manage and control yourself and your life.

 Either you become a human being or you live as an exploited human biomass, loved by the mad leaders of all big mega corporations and institutions. There is no paradise without being a human! You decide!

7. Build up your Ideals, Values, Norms and Rules

👍 *Ideals, values, norms and rules must be founded in the human values.*

👍 *Ideals, values, norms and rules must be balanced for the entire humanity.*

👍 *Ideals, values, norms and rules must consider the environment and nature.*

👍 *Ideals, values, norms and rules must promote the archetypal evolution.*

👍 *Ideals, values, norms and rules must promote Individuation for everybody.*

👍 *Ideals, values, norms and rules must be founded in the Archetypes of the Soul.*

Adjectives that express positive qualities (values):

Humanistic, spiritual, archetypal, ideal, authentic, truthful, peaceful, hopeful, fair, strong, effective, balanced, healthy, flexible, realistic, practical, useful, sociable, etc.

→ From today on, all humans practice self-knowledge and self-education.

→ From today on, all humans learn about love, relationship, marriage, and family life.

→ From today on, all humans learn to interpret their dreams and to live with the inner Spirit.

→ From today on, all humans practice "living in the process of Individuation".

→ From today on, all humans learn how to educate children with respect for their inner life.

→ All humans respect and strive for fulfillment of the Archetypes of the Soul.

 Either you become a human being or you live as an exploited human biomass, loved by the mad leaders of all big mega corporations and institutions. There is no paradise without being a human! You decide!

8. Achieve Balanced Success

👍 *To become professionally successful, and at the same time to live with love and the inner Spirit, that is success!*

👍 *To reach a powerful leadership position, and at the same time respecting humanity, that is success!*

👍 *To rule the world with the inner Spirit, and globally promote Individuation, that is success!*

👍 *To live the truth, together with the Archetypes of the Soul, that is success!*

👍 *To be a spiritual guide, who has fulfilled the corresponding Archetypes, that is success!*

👍 *To live with an all-sided balanced life philosophy, with the Archetypes of the Soul, that is success!*

Get success with yourself:

Your being: Positive emotional state, health, wellbeing, joy of life, happiness, peace, trust, inner harmony, energetic balance, satisfaction, protection, authenticity, autonomy, self-realization, realization of talents and interests, and complete fulfillment.

Your life: Work, study, learning, knowledge, career, business, relationship, marriage, family life, social life, education of your children, holidays, leisure, solving problems, creative activities, personal life culture, etc.

→ Yes, you can have complete success with yourself, your life!

Form yourself in the psychical-spiritual functions: perception, interpretation, learning, will, self-identity, ego-strength, defense mechanisms, projection, intelligence, thinking, love, inner genuine needs, unconscious mind, moral character, etc.

 Either you achieve balanced success or you live with pollution, contamination (soil, air, water, sea, and food), environmental destruction, crimes, violence, cheat, lies, falseness, climate change, financial crisis, exorbitant exploitation, wars, militarization, fascism, etc. Not a good life without success! Find balance or forget about Paradise. You decide!

9. Find your Personal New Life Style

👍 *A personal life style is always related to its consequences.*

👍 *You will harvest from the way you live.*

👍 *The way you live today programs your future.*

👍 *The consequences of your way of living are seen thousands of miles away.*

👍 *The future generations inherit all the direct and lateral effects of the way you live today.*

Some orientations to balance your way of living:

→ Smoke 20% less and drink 20% less alcohol.

→ Consume 20% less petrol and use 20% less electricity.

→ Reduce the amount of meat and fish that you consume by 20%.

→ Use 20% less water (when you shower, wash clothes, etc.).

→ Reduce heating and A/C costs (gas, oil, electricity) by 20%.

→ Don't buy goods with consumer credit or personal loans.

→ Get cash from the bank or the ATM of your bank.

→ Eat 20% less snacks and drink 20% less beer while watching TV.

→ Go shopping to your local market or local shops.

→ Reduce your monthly pocket money by 20%.

→ Buy 20% less newspapers and magazines.

→ Spend 20% less money: 20% less goods/20% cheaper goods.

→ Perfume/Toiletry: use 20% less or buy 20% cheaper.

→ Use detergents sparingly and you easily save 20%

→ Use medicine when it is really appropriate and save 20%

→ Go to a hairdresser, beauty salon, gym that is 20% cheaper

→ Turn off appliances at home (TV, PC, Radio) when not used

→ Watch 20% less TV every day

→ Use your mobile phone 20% less and reduce talking by 20%

→ Use your computer (e.g. surfing the internet, chatting) 20% less

→ Buy a small present for your partner and kids every week

→ Read one book about humans, life, and the earth every month.

 Either you find and live your new personal life style, or you waste a lot of money which you will need in the future. Not a good life with blind materialism and later poverty and misery! There is no paradise for blind sheep and brainwashed consumers. You decide!

10. Contribute Towards a Better Humanity and Earth

👍 *You want a good future for yourself.*

👍 *You want a good future for your children.*

👍 *You want a good future for the coming generations.*

👍 *You want a good future for humanity and the earth.*

→ You must be responsible for your future, the future of your children and the youth today, and for the future of humanity and the planet!

With your "consumer behavior" you can contribute a lot:

- Eat healthy food instead of taking vitamin and mineral supplements.
- Buy quality products that last for a long time.
- Buy bio-products and in general focus more on natural decorations
- Inform yourself by consulting consumer information.
- Buy agricultural products from your area (local markets)
- Before procreating a baby, learn about care, budgets, education.
- Before getting married, learn about relationships (courses).

- Buy a home with maximum 50% mortgage and a long term interest rate.
- Only buy a holiday home with cash; never with a mortgage.
- Buy your car with maximum 35% (50%) credit for 3 years.
- Invest your money in 100% secure offers and avoid speculations.
- Invest periodically in further education for life and job/work.
- Invest money in books (DVDs) with high learning potentials.
- Support local businesses by buying their products.
- Go back to the old times, pay for everything you buy in cash.
- Benefit regularly from the holiday offers in your own country.
- Never sign a contract you have not read carefully and slept over.
- Never accept conditions that you don't agree with fully.
- Don't live the life of people you see on TV; live your life.
- Eat with time and style, and celebrate eating with others.

 Either you contribute for a better humanity and earth, or you will pay a fortune for the personal and collective damages in the future! It is a soulless life with an unconscious way of consuming and living; the door to paradise will not open. You decide!

11. Always Ask Questions

👍 *The most critical question is: Who am I?*

👍 *The most useful question is: What are the motives of my actions?*

👍 *The most delicate question is: Who speaks the truth?*

👍 *Another indispensable question is: What is hidden behind people's façades, words, and actions?*

👍 *And the most important question is: What am I on this earth for?*

Not asking such questions means being ignorant, disrespectful, irresponsible, indifferent, dumb, and lazy. The behavior of such people is inefficient and thoroughly destructive towards humanity and the earth.

The indispensable orientations:
➡ Acquire as much knowledge as you can to get answers.
➡ Your dreams tell you the truth; the inner Spirit knows everything.
➡ Be decisive when searching as well as honest and critical with yourself.
➡ All answers start with the reality of your mind.
➡ Your psychical-spiritual development leads to the right answers.
➡ Follow the Archetypes of the Soul to get on the right path.

→ With correct meditation you discover inner worlds and meanings.

→ Critically control your way of perceiving, thinking, judging.

→ Always look behind the scenes, games, façades and masks.

→ Always identify the effects that something has for life and people.

→ Multiply a fact, effect, or action by billions and you see the value.

→ Close your eyes and you can see the real reality and the truth.

→ In the result of a behavior you can see the qualities and motives.

→ Recognize your entire inner life, and compare with answers.

→ Find out if what others say and teach is comprehensible.

 Either you ask such highly important questions and try to find the right answers, or you remain brainwashed and manipulated! There is no paradise for those that don't search for genuine answers. You decide!

12. Understand Your Behavior and the Way you Act

👍 *You can act efficiently and get the right result with your behavior.*

👍 *Acting can be good, useful, constructive, promoting, deliberating, satisfying.*

👍 *Acting can be meaningless, dangerous, bad, evil, embarrassing, damaging.*

👍 *Each action also expresses a value or quality in reference to the result.*

👍 *A life without reflected behavior and acting is a very poor life.*

👍 *Acting blindly driven by emotions, greed, or drive destroys life and the planet.*

Thoroughly reflect your behavior and acting under the right perspectives:

➔ Acting is future-oriented, aim-oriented, by purpose, potentially conscious.

➔ Actions contain: process, a level of complexity, and a situation.

➔ The process: starting phase, course, and final act.

→ Phases of action contain: emotional, structural and energetic aspects.

→ Acting often goes together with the use of measures.

→ Effects of acting (desired or not) can be identified.

→ Actions can be judged (evaluated) and the actor called to account.

→ Elements of a situation can become a psychological impact for the action.

→ Achieving the desired aim or failure creates a self-feeling.

→ Culture is objectification of actions.

Either you reflect and understand your behavior and acting, or you will never get satisfaction, success, and fulfillment! Not to consider being responsible for the motives and results of behavior is a miserable way of living. There is no paradise for irresponsible people. You decide!

13. Live in an Evolutionary Way

🖐 *If a society is created by evolutionary human beings, then one can see the result in the environment and society.*

🖐 *Live on the path to self-knowledge and your self-fulfillment!*

The essential characteristics are:
- Accept the psychical life and consciously form all forces.
- Liberate yourself from inner burdens of your biography.
- Become free from projection and rigid defense mechanisms.
- Constructively elaborate and transform images in the unconscious.
- Find inner orientation through dream interpretation and meditation.
- Integrate and elaborate all the uncomfortable "things" in life.
- Create relationships and life from Individuation.
- Deal with nature and the environment with Spirit and love.
- Develop and use the power of love with sophistication.
- Be flexible and with inner freedom towards material goods.
- Give highest value to psychical-spiritual performances.

Live with love and Spirit and be decisive and firm:
→ Reject ego-centrism, narcissism, self-satisfaction and

arrogance.

→ Reject emptiness, perversion, psychopaths, hate, greed, lack of Spirit and balance.

→ Reject narrow-mindedness, naivety, ignorance, stubbornness, and blindness.

→ Reject living a life pushed by your drive, coded by your unpurged unconscious.

→ Reject living a life without love and Spirit, and ignoring genuine inner needs.

→ Reject falseness, games, intrigues, lies, self-lies, and life lies.

→ Reject the dogmatic and spiritual market that offers you over 10,000 meanders.

 Either you live evolutionary, or you will perish with the billions of people that live beyond psychical-spiritual evolution! Not to forget that a lack of genuine spirituality in the collective leads to war and fascism; and in the future it destroys humanity and the planet. There is no paradise for people that live an archaic understanding of humans. You decide!

14. Live Solidarity for Individuation

👍 *A global Individuation which follows the path of the Archetypal processes of the Soul is the incredible solution for humanity and the earth!*

👍 *Individuation includes the spiritual understanding of human beings and meaning of life for religions as well as for politics.*

👍 *Individuation is the indispensable psychical-spiritual path for all officials in all religions and every concept of Spirituality.*

👍 *Individuation is the collective path of salvation! A concept that can be lived in all cultural expressions.*

Individuation is the ultimate understanding of human being and human life. Individuation is the new mankind for the third Millennium:

➔ It is a disgrace not to thoroughly practice self-knowledge.

➔ It is a disgrace not to live with love and the inner Spirit.

➔ It is a disgrace not to consider the formation of human's inner life.

➔ It is a disgrace not to respect the Archetypes of the Soul.

➔ It is a disgrace to be religious without the Archetypes of the Soul.

→ It is a disgrace to be a political leader without the inner Spirit.

→ It is a disgrace to marry and not to practice Individuation.

→ It is a disgrace to abuse the Archetype of marriage.

→ It is a disgrace to procreate a baby and not to consider its soul.

→ It is a disgrace to consume and focus on materialism without soul.

→ It is a disgrace to scrupulously push billions of people into poverty.

→ It is a disgrace to want to establish a world order.

→ It is a disgrace to exorbitantly exploit the resources.

→ It is a disgrace to rule the world with lunacy and religious psychosis.

 Either you live Individuation and grow towards the archetypal aim of the complete fulfillment, or you will completely fail with your life on earth! Not to consider the psychical-spiritual development and not making the best of it is a disgrace and shameful waste of human life. There is no paradise for people that live such a disgrace! You decide!

15. Practice Holistic Self-knowledge

☝ *To constructively and effectively manage yourself you must know yourself very well.*

☝ *You cannot ignore what and how you are with your psyche and expect to know what other people are.*

☝ *The better you know yourself, the more truthful, trustworthy and reliable you are.*

☝ *The more you develop yourself psychologically and spiritually, the better you know yourself.*

☝ *Self-knowledge is also a conscious way of living every day.*

Self-knowledge includes all psychical-spiritual functions:
- You must think profoundly, in networks, and with knowledge.
- You must know when and why you have certain feelings.
- You must be able to understand and deal with feelings.
- You must satisfy your inner needs with love, Spirit, intelligence.
- You must know about your love as a manifold potential.
- You must know how to center and strengthen your energy.
- You must know who you are and what you are, your inner Self.

- You must be the captain of your entire being and life.

- You must know your ideals, attitudes, beliefs, values and norms.

- You must have a strong will and clearly reasoned aims and wishes.

- You must flexibly control your defense mechanisms.

- You must control what you integrate from the world.

- You must precisely perceive, long-sighted, and interrelated.

- You must correctly interpret your dreams and benefit from them.

- You must use meditation and fantasies as a creative source.

- You must know the inventory that is piled up in your unconscious.

- You must have a lot of information and knowledge about life.

- You must constructively make use of knowledge.

- You must extensively form your skills for living and mastering life.

 Either you practice holistic self-knowledge, or you will be treated as a human-like animal! There is no paradise for blind people that ignore self-knowledge and therefore are unable to manage themselves! You decide!

16. Live with the Archetypes of the Soul

👍 *With the Archetypes of the Soul you have the absolute guarantee to go the right path and to achieve the authentic, complete fulfillment.*

👍 *The indispensable patterns (models, steps) in this psychological-spiritual growing process ("Individuation") are the Archetypes of the Soul.*

These are the Archetypes of the Soul for the psychical-spiritual development:

→ Accepting and turning to the whole inner life

→ Discovering and forming all inner forces

→ Developing the true Self by conscious forming

→ Integrating the inner Spirit as guidance

→ Proceedings of dying and becoming new

→ Unification with the inner opposite gender pole

→ Integration of the spiritual principles

→ Balance between external and internal life

→ Fulfillment of the completeness and wholeness.

→ Find genuine happiness, fulfillment and get into the paradise

- You must understand the content and dynamics of your unconscious.

- You must elaborate heavy and hindering biographical aspects.

- You must become new from the bottom of your being.

- You must transform the opposites, imbalances and shadows.

- You must become free from unconscious complexes and conflicts.

- You must form the balance of the polarity to the other gender.

- You must grow to an all-sided balanced unity and totality.

- You must live with love, Spirit, mind, intelligence, wisdom, and skills.

- You must elaborate the archetypal processes of Individuation.

- You must understand Individuation as a way of living and growing.

 Either you live with the Archetypes of the Soul, or you live on earth like in the archaic hell! There is no paradise for blind people that ignore the Archetypes of the Soul! You decide!

17. Live with all your Inner Potentials

👍 *Everybody must live with intelligence, love, wisdom, knowledge, skills and methods, and the inner Spirit!*

- You must accept love as an important and essential life force.
- Professors and teachers must want wisdom; students must want wisdom.
- Everybody must take self-knowledge seriously.
- All people win with the truth, with love, the inner Spirit.
- All people go as far as to say "feelings are important".
- Men and women respect that they have genuine inner needs.
- All people on earth will become 50% healthier.
- Car owners must drive 50% less.
- All households and enterprises consume 50% less electricity.
- Every adult pursues one hour of self-knowledge every day.
- Every teacher and professor has worked through their biography.
- Every human must immediately reduce his waste by 50%.
- All politicians don't lie and don't distort anymore.
- Statesmen and ministers must become "individuated humans".
- Adults reflect on their leisure, use it with mind and soul.

- Nobody is a fan of high-performance sport, but still of sport.

- Everybody wants to learn after school and vocational school.

- All adults must read 12 books every year about the psychical life.

- Every day all newspapers must report about the dreams of their readers.

- Everybody has to practice self-knowledge before getting married.

- It is forbidden to have children without a thorough self-education.

- Only people who live with the inner Spirit can become a boss.

- All adults practice meditation for 10 minutes twice daily.

- Everybody writes on their door, what makes them happy.

→ Develop new visions for yourself and for humanity in the future!

→ Start with a completely new understanding of human life!

→ You can only win if most people on earth also want to win!

 Either you make a positive network of life culture work, or you do not deserve to be on earth! There is no paradise for people that reject a new understanding of a human way of living! You decide!

18. Succeed with Self-management

👍 *Everybody must live with an efficient self-management!*

👍 *Even children can and must learn self-management!*

→ You need time for yourself. Nobody has to be reachable and accessible at every time of the day.

→ To say "no" without frustrating the other person, is an art. On the other hand one has to be able to say "yes" as well.

→ Identifying troubles gives us a clear orientation. Strategies for problem solving make life easier.

→ Think and act with an aim in mind: In daily life, plan and act in the perspective of long term personal aims.

→ Aspire for your determined aims with a timetable and with working methods. Sometimes reading a book can help achieve that.

→ Divide the big aims of life into small constructive steps. Each life phase has its own goals. Ensure that you never miss out on living the present!

→ Prestige, money and success are not the highest aims of life! Reflect upon your consumption, your compensating behavior.

→ Concentrate on the use of your energy. Don't dissipate your forces through chaos and lack of planning. Recharge your energy.

→ Ascertain priorities, which lead to determined aims. The truthful life is the essential aim of life. Working is also living.

→ Not everything is equally important and urgent. Importance means: aim and success. Urgency means: time and fixed date.

→ Deal with daily matters, but also with long term goals and aims. Where do you want to be in 1-3 years, in 5-10 years?

→ Regularly control your use of time. Make a day to day plan for the week, integrating your use of time.

→ Control your stress factors in order for them not to control you. There are hundreds of stress factors in daily life.

 Either you learn and practice an efficient self-management, or your life will be and end in a chaos! There is no paradise for people without an efficient self-management! You decide!

19. Manage your Time Efficiently

👍 *Don't waste 20-25 years of your lifetime for meaningless activities.*

👍 *A constructive control of time usage gives your life quality.*

Some orientations to consider about time management:

→ Recognize time wasters

→ Plan the day in the morning

→ Check through your daily aims

→ Communicate awake and clear

→ Organize dossiers and files

→ Prepare telephone calls

→ Define small aims for the day

→ Start acting slowly

→ Make checklists

→ Say "no" if appropriate

→ Recognize urgency

→ Recognize importance

→ Don't always hesitate

→ Make a shopping list

→ Reflect on mobility

→ Concentrate while talking

→ Take breaks

→ Overview courses

→ Respect your biorhythm

→ Structure your preparations

→ Explore before you plan

→ Plan before you act

→ Analyze your daily time use

You are not allowed to spend 20-25 years in front of the television, waiting in traffic jams, doing nothing, acting inefficiently, talking nonsense, picking your nose, and mocking life!

 Either you learn an efficient time-management, or you lose 20-25% of your lifetime! There is no paradise for people that lose a lot of life time! You decide!

20. Practice Efficient Life Techniques

👍 *Efficiency is the balanced result of using life techniques.*

👍 *Life techniques are more than "techniques", but also an expression of the formed personality.*

Apply the basic rules of life techniques:

→ Follow the principles of small steps.

→ Elaborate information carefully.

→ Dose the amount and the intensity.

→ Consciously practice self-management.

→ Think positively with intelligence.

→ Accept diligence and effort for success.

→ Control your perception.

→ Think in an all-sided network.

→ Give value in an extended context.

→ Live your genuine human being.

Practice life techniques:

▪ Concentrate on the result of your acting.

▪ Invest time and work for your life wishes.

▪ Explore the way of your thinking and judging.

▪ Determine aims and take responsibility for success.

- Try to resolve problems objectively and with intelligence.
- Distinguish between importance and urgency.
- Calculate the required time for a specific matter.
- Leave space in your time planning for unexpected matters.
- Use your time in the best efficient way.
- Build up a strong and sane self-confidence.
- Give high importance to your genuine needs.
- Take responsibility for your feelings and moods.
- Build up strength and consider your weaknesses.
- Act and courageously dare to deal with something new.
- Elaborate without delay pending tasks and duties.

 Either you learn and practice life techniques, or your life will be a failure with endless suffering, quarrels and mushroomed problems! There is no paradise for people that ignore life techniques! You decide!

21. Build up Happiness

👉 *You must do a lot with yourself and your life to become happy.*

- You must live your true being, your potentials and talents.
  Find out what your genuine inner being is.

- You must live meaning, values, and human qualities.
  Find your values and your meaning.

- You must grow and develop yourself as an authentic person.
  Explore yourself and your inner life.

- You must live, give, and receive love, and create joy of life.
  Learn about the many-sided power of love.

- You must know, think, and conclude and judge correctly.
  Simply learn by reading books and articles.

- You must live a relationship including sex, constructively.
  Learn to be able to do so.

- You must care for your psychical and physical health.
  Live truthful in order to be psychically healthy.

- You must act efficiently in daily matters.
  Learn life techniques and the right methods.

- You must have balance and stability in life.
  Openness and flexibility is the key for balance.

- You must form autonomy and self-determination.
Clean what is brainwashed and don't let yourself be brainwashed.

- You must experience God and the transcendence inside.
The only way to do so is to grow and to develop yourself.

- You must be guided by the inner Spirit.
This is possible with dream interpretation and meditation.

 Either you learn how to be and become happy, or your life will be overshadowed by sadness, sorrow, and emptiness! There is no paradise for people that reject happiness! You decide!

22. Your Interests of Utmost Importance

👍 *Don't let yourself be driven by curiosity for empty and meaningless interests just to turn away from yourself!*

👍 *Don't direct your interest for "things" that are none of your business*

👍 *Direct your drive for interest towards human values, human life, and meaningful personal aims!*

👍 *Always give maximum attention and care to your genuine interests!*

Become aware of your genuine and meaningful interests:

a) Interest to know: Curiosity, drive to understand, tendency to dedication, thirst to know, need to integrate, consciousness about our creation, love for life, experiences, having an overview.

b) Interest to act: drive to create, to act, to form, to use, to care, to manage, to educate, to realize plans, to develop, to live consciously, to live culture.

c) Interest in being happy: Lust, joy, love, hope, satisfaction, wisdom, wellness, fulfillment, self-realization (of all potentials).

d) Interest in becoming a human: Personality education (forming personality) and Individuation as the inner process of growth in the psychical and spiritual dimension (evolution).

e) Become yourself:

→ Become authentic, completely yourself!

→ Live what you truly are inside!

→ Find the valuable self that you are inside!

→ Modernize everything that there is to revise!

→ Live from your healthy psychical forces!

→ Use your life forces for a genuine life!

→ Build up genuine fulfillment from the inside!

 Either you form and direct your interests towards meaningful activities, or you and your life are a boring monkey-like existence! There is no paradise for people that ignore their genuine interests! You decide!

23. Satisfy your Genuine Inner Needs

👍 *You are responsible to satisfy your inner needs.*

Self-love: self-knowledge, self-exploration, exploring the personal world, self-forming, peace and harmony with oneself

Love: true love, honesty, respect, fairness, care, physical nearness (relationship), joy of life, happiness, hope

Relationship: sex with love and tenderness, sharing life with a partner of the opposite sex, understanding the other gender

Marriage: faithfulness, living the male-female balance, sharing existence, and growing together

Family: (being) a good father, (being) a good mother, having one's own family, being responsible for family and children

Home: warm-hearted home, emotional safety (protection), physical safety (protection), care for the emotional home (well-being)

Personality: authentic expression, authentic self-confidence, authentic self-esteem, a positive authentic self-identity

Development: understanding one's own being, growing (psychical-spiritual development), developing and living talents

Spirituality: a spiritual rootedness, a spiritual orientation, spiritual experiences, fulfillment of all longing, complete fulfillment

Education: education (from family), education (school), education (professional perspectives), education (personal, life)

Work: work (working), being adequately paid for work, performing something special, responsibility, talents and professional abilities

Social: social attention, a positive social environment, social celebrations, democratic rules, cooperation, peace and justice

Environment: a healthy natural environment, a healthy living environment, healthy food and drinking water, experiencing nature

Leisure: playing, games, fun, entertainment, pleasure, humor, sport (physical) activities, creative activities, living and creating culture

 Either you satisfy your genuine inner needs, or you live as an empty, superficial, consuming human biomass! There is no paradise for those that are human biomass who ignore their genuine inner needs! You decide!

24. Find a New Understanding about your Health

 ☛ *Health is an expression of life culture.*

 ☛ *Health includes the inner life and spiritual values.*

 ☛ *Health is a way of living, is realization of life, and is a way of mastering life.*

Find a new understanding of "health":

→ Health is a complete bodily, psychical and social well-being and not only the absence of illness and disease.

→ Health is a culture of all means of life; health is assimilation of body and environment through social actions; health is a way of living.

→ Factors of health are also methodical principles such as 'aspire for appropriateness', 'respond to feelings', and 'nearness to life'.

→ Self-responsibility and self-determination are an important part of a healthy personality development.

→ Health is understood as a part of the individual life course development and with that a conscious way of living.

The essential factors that form health include:

- Productivity, creativity, being active, working, thinking
- The objective-rational contact with the reality
- Adaptability, internal balance, ego-integration
- Ability to satisfy genuine inner needs, including sexuality
- Being free from (or limited) use of defense mechanism
- Tolerance of frustration, strengthened against stress
- Realistic definition of aims, orientation in meaning and values
- Balance between stability and flexibility
- Realization of individual potentials and talents
- Realistic self-image, self-acceptance, self-esteem, self-confidence
- Naturalness, spontaneity, sociability, genuineness, free from lies
- Openness for new experiences and feelings, mind-expanding
- Aiming for the 'good', the truth, the beauty

 Either you get a new understanding of health, or you risk unnecessary and unforeseeable suffering! There is no paradise for people that ignore matters of health as part of a way of living and growing! You decide!

25. Form the Strength of your Personality

👍 *It is outstanding to be a rock-solid, strong and all-sided balanced personality.*

👍 *Forming and understanding all psychical forces and their interplay gives inner strength.*

👍 *The eternal key to a strong personality lies in the Archetypes of the Soul.*

👍 *To become such a valuable personality there are some essential points to take into consideration.*

The essence of a strong personality:

→ You need relevant knowledge and information about life

→ You must form broad perception with realistic interpretation

→ You must become able to think carefully and in networks

→ You must practice self-critical contemplation and thinking

→ You must control defense mechanisms and projection

→ You must form realistic ideals and aims with human values

→ You must form a realistic self-identity with strong self-confidence

→ You must build up will power and clear rooted motivation

→ You must form skills to master life, including

communication

→ You must develop an efficient self-management and self-control

→ You must respect genuine needs, emotional life, and life energy

→ You must learn skills to solve crises, problems and conflicts

→ You must use intuition, creativity, meditation, and your dreams

→ You must not suppress or ignore the content of your unconscious

→ You must be responsible towards nature and the resources

→ You must form your meaning of life and your positive character

→ You must apply efficient rules, norms, measures, and attitudes

→ You must form a balance of your inner male-female polarity

 Either you build up a strong personality, or you will get abused, exploited, oppressed, ignored, and you will not have success in your life! There is no paradise for people that do not build up a strong personality! You decide!

26. Make your Perception Work

👍 *Thinking, talking and behavior start with perception.*

👍 *You can only get success with the right perception.*

👍 *Your thinking can't be better than your perception.*

👍 *Always thoroughly consider your patterns of interpretation.*

👍 *Learn to make your perception efficient:*

Think critically about the way your perception works:

- Clear, objective, precise, awake
- Manifold, all-embracing, differentiated, deep
- In clear order, precisely classified
- Flexible, mobile in a broader field
- Far-reaching, with time perspective (past, future)
- Responsible, considerate, purposeful
- With clear value-experience, free from prejudgment
- Assimilating, integrating, revealing, unfolding

Become aware of your subjective perception:

→ The reality you have in your mind is a simplified, manipulated, subjective world.

→ The meaning and value you give to a reality depends on your biography.

→ You select, accentuate, filter, reduce, and manipulate the elements of your perception.

→ Your interpretation also reflects the spirit of the society (zeitgeist, pressure).

→ You interpret with emotions, opinions, prejudgments, and with plausibility.

→ You interpret with your ideology, dogmatism, moral, values, and norms.

 Either you become aware of your way of perceiving and interpreting, or you will be a victim of social pressure, wrong patterns of interpretation, and illusions! There is no paradise for people that do not critically reflect their perception and interpretation of perceived realities! You decide!

27. Pay Attention to the Quality and Efficiency of your Thinking

👍 *Think carefully and considerately in order to get good results.*

👍 *Look at the state of humanity and the earth, and you will see how little people think.*

👍 *Most people talk faster than they can think; the result is garbage for the rubbish bin.*

Learn how to think efficiently:

→ Always keep in mind: thinking is a strenuous performance.

→ Efficient thinking requires a rich vocabulary, a skilful language.

→ To be free from unconscious complexes increases the objectivity of thinking.

→ Combine logical thinking and complex analysis with a meditative approach.

→ Use your intuition, your creativity and associations to get useful results.

→ Structure your knowledge, your information and your thoughts.

→ Use the right information to get efficient results from your thinking.

→ Consider your emotional state and your inner needs when thinking.

→ Be aware of your aims, values, and judgments when thinking.

→ Recognize interrelations, networks, and hidden realities when thinking.

→ Understand realities with flexible patterns of interpretation and varied views.

→ With attitudes of love and with your dreams your thinking becomes balanced.

Do you know that most people absolutely do not think about anything important with knowledge, skills and the right perception?

 Either you learn to think efficiently and critically, or the result of your thinking becomes a life long nightmare: an inefficient acting and way of living that produces enormous problems! There is no paradise for people that do not learn to think efficiently and critically! You decide!

28. Regularly Care for your Mental Fitness

👍 *Mental fitness makes your thinking and acting efficient.*

👍 *Mental fitness is the indispensable condition for a good third age.*

👍 *Mental fitness has a decisive function in personal and professional areas for satisfaction, success, and fulfillment.*

👍 *Mental fitness can be trained and used on a daily basis.*

Some important suggestions to consider:

- Write down what you said and what the other person said after a phone call.
- Preview the day and plan the coming day imaginatively and by thinking.
- Go through the previous day and experience the situations again.
- Work through difficult situations thoroughly and write down the key elements.
- Keep a diary about your experiences, about others and all kinds of subjects.
- Write down your dreams, work through them, draw diagrams, and play with sceneries.
- Communicate feelings; express them physically and with

constructive actions.

- Handle and plan creatively: visits, festivities, presents, rituals, being together.

Mental fitness happens through confrontation with life:

→ Precisely elaborate conflicts and guide them towards solutions.

→ Precisely formulate your own values, revise them if necessary.

→ Look behind masks and facades; find a clear view for depth.

→ See life in a complex network; don't naively simplify things.

→ Learn new things steadily through systematically aimed reading.

→ Consciously deal with your life-time and your forces.

 Either you regularly train your mental fitness, or you will mentally become "an old and boring person" with a very stubborn character! There is no paradise for stubborn and mentally dull people! You decide!

29. Use your Intelligence Every Day

☝ *Use the potential of your intelligence.*

☝ *Using intelligence provides success.*

☝ *Thinking expresses the quality of your intelligence.*

First of all learn the basics:

→ Look behind the masks and façades of others.

→ Learn to like to read texts with serious content.

→ Practice expressing yourself clearly.

→ Decompose complex matters into parts.

→ Consciously control what you want to perceive.

→ Be thorough when analyzing a problem.

→ Have a good retentiveness.

→ Never strangle your thinking with dogmas and ideologies.

→ Reflect upon your values and norms.

→ Cautiously examine your beliefs.

→ Think before you judge.

→ Justify your demands.

→ Be flexible in integrating something new.

→ Think in complex networks.

→ Perceive with the perspective of time.

→ Reflect your attitudes thoroughly.

You have your intelligence! Regardless of having a low or high IQ, simply use what you have in your brain! Your IQ level is not the problem.

YOU are the problem: Don't be lazy, dull, arrogant, a bigmouth, blinded by religious psychosis, or driven by a shopping addiction and arrogant narcissism.

If stupidity would smell like sewage, then most people would be poisoning the environment, contaminating the air and soil, and lose all their friends.

 Either you use your intelligence, or you form part of the stupid creatures, a being without future on this earth! Not thinking profoundly destroys humanity and the earth! There is no paradise for dull, lazy-minded, and arrogant people! You decide!

30. Learn to Read Efficiently

👍 *Every week, you need to read about important life issues.*

👍 *Read efficiently and learn efficiently for your life.*

Learn about reading:

→ First of all you need to get a general idea about the content of a book and the text of your interest. You do not start reading every word.

→ You first need to adapt the text material to your purposes and interest. Read through the table of contents (chapters), the foreword and the index. You can then read the first and last paragraph of each chapter.

→ Also take a look at any diagrams and figures included in the book. From all this you may get about 20-30% of the meaning.

→ In the next step you find out specific details of the topic of your interest. There is no need to read a whole book for this purpose.

→ Identify the key words that cover your subject or questions. Main step: Some subjects require a very detailed understanding.

→ Now your selected reading becomes more time consuming. Underline, highlight and use the margins for your comments or questions.

→ Go through the texts again and summarize the essential content onto small cards with a keyword each. You need to understand the essential terms, facts, theses, and theories.

→ You also need to understand the course of arguing and the network of the knowledge and theories. Always read critically, ask questions, compare facts with other facts, and especially contemplate the given conclusions.

It's an incredible shame that every month you spend money for mobile phones, nightlife, going out, petrol, your car, interest for bank loans, etc, but you don't want to spend not even a bit money for a good book to stimulate your personal development to master life!

 Either you read books and articles, or you are a mere burden to humanity! Not profoundly reading books, informing yourself about humans and life, destroys humanity and the earth! Such a life is shit that contaminates the earth. There is no paradise for such stupid people! You decide!

31. Never Stop Learning

👍 *Pay attention to the components that support learning.*

👍 *Learn with a prepared frame and preparation.*

👍 *Learning is part of life; you must learn during your whole life!*

→ Learn free from external pressure, find stimulation to learn, motivate yourself to learn, activate your lust to explore and your curiosity, find an interest, and have positive feelings towards knowledge.

→ Accept effort and discipline; take responsibility for the learning process, build up confidence in your ability to learn, accept your learning deficit; adapt new learning situations and frustration.

→ Manage your learning: take on the responsibility to learn, organize your learning, plan dealing with pauses, control your energy and motivation, and see the importance of knowledge and learning.

→ Learn to endure antagonisms and contradictions, accept suffering by trying to understand and to find the right thoughts, be perseverant in abstract thinking and ready for changes in attitudes.

Favorable learning dispositions include:

- Attitudes for learning, principally being ready to learn.
- Ability to organize learning situations and to manage them.
- Interest in knowledge and creativity in psychical fields.
- Perseverance, endurance and the ability to concentrate.
- Clear perception, mental presence, perspicacious thinking.
- Positive acceptance of life problems and challenges.
- Readiness to recognize and understand psychical realities.
- Interest in a differentiated development and growth process.
- Dedication to values such as truthfulness and love.

How can you be so stupid to not want to learn during your whole life? Be humble and accept that you do not know anything about humans, human life, the mystery of humans, the truth about humans, the meaning of life, about love, the Archetypes of the Soul, and the inner Spirit.

Believe in ideologies and dogmas, follow the religious psychosis and you will completely lose your life!

 Either you care for success in learning, or you will be lost! There is no paradise for stubborn, naïve and lazy-minded people! You decide!

32. Learn about Efficient Learning

👍 *Every week you need to learn something about life and about how life works.*

👍 *Every day until your last day you need to learn about humans and the damages they produce.*

👍 *You need to learn how to live efficiently and to achieve your fulfillment.*

Learn about learning:

Everybody learns and has started learning since their prenatal time. Learning means acquiring new knowledge, behaviors and skills, values and attitudes. Learning starts with understanding words, terms, theories, and networks of facts. Adapting new behavior and skills may need special training.

Personal psychical-spiritual development is a learning process. Learning can be goal-oriented or can happen by accident in any life situation. Learning occurs by studying, copying, playing, or simply through an unaware adaptation or by "trial and error". Motivation and positive learning attitudes enormously facilitate the learning process.

Organize your learning: What do I want to learn? What do I want to achieve? Why do I want to achieve this determined goal? Where do I find what I should learn?

Then you need to make your timetable: set the main goal into small parts and small goals; learn with the corresponding small steps. Give the necessary priority and appropriate study time to this learning in your daily life. Consider your biorhythm for learning! Make a weekly and monthly study plan.

Make your notes and revise the entire work periodically, every week. Write down graphics (diagrams, tables, mind-maps, etc.) and summaries of the parts of the subject on small cards. Add new content, ideas and connections that occur to you in the process to the summaries you've made.

 Either you learn, and learn how to efficiently learn, or you remain an archaic human being, abused and exploited from all sides! There is no paradise for such stupid people! You decide!

33. Live the Power of Love

👍 *Love is of highest importance!*

👍 *Live love every day!*

👍 *First of all, love yourself!*

👍 *Acquire the right understanding of love!*

👍 *Love is the specific essential human nature.*

👍 *Love is the deepest meaning of life.*

Live love every day:

➔ Love is a many-sided creative force of life.

➔ Love gives meaning and value to life.

➔ Love makes life worth living and rich.

➔ Love is a creative force for the daily life.

➔ Love is the key to a lot of apparently unsolvable situations.

➔ Love respects life's many-sided balances.

➔ Love respects life in manifold ways.

➔ Love is a complex performance.

➔ Love without thinking has got a very small chance for success.

➔ Love without the inner Spirit is structure-less, has no inner roots.

➔ Love demands to precisely look at the genuine inner needs.

→ Love understands all-sided balanced human beings.

→ Love demands the psychical-spiritual development.

→ Love consciously perceives the future above the quick pleasure.

→ Love has got a tendency to form a balanced inner wholeness.

→ Through self-love one is able to live love in real life.

- It is a disgrace how people ignore to live the power of love.

- It is a disgrace how people ignore to seek for the truth.

- It is a disgrace how people treat children without love.

- It is a disgrace how most politicians are unable to love.

- It is a disgrace how Christianity teaches love together with lies.

 Either you learn to love and live love every day, or you will spend your life as an instinctive, archaic human being, with a permanent destructive and evil dynamic! There is no paradise for such love-less people! You decide!

34. Live Love with your Partner

👍 *I love you with heart, body, mind, Spirit and soul.*

👍 *I love you from the bottom of my being.*

👍 *I love you with knowledge, wisdom and skills.*

👍 *I love you with full trust and faith.*

👍 *I love you with intelligence, reason, intuition and body feelings.*

👍 *I love you without hidden reserve and without limit.*

You must live love every day!

→ Give high value to truthfulness and reliability in your life.

→ Promote mutual care of the psychical-spiritual life.

→ Turn towards emotions and interpret feelings as a message.

→ Face the facts of life with responsibility and awareness.

→ Develop the potentials and promote them with your partner.

→ Express sensuality in diverse ways with your partner.

→ Take arguments seriously and reconcile the same day.

→ Initiate constructive talks often and talk about small daily matters.

→ Creatively live your sexual drive as much as possible together.

→ Only procreate a baby if you are prepared for the

challenges.

→ If you don't want a baby avoid creating a baby with all measures.

→ Express signs of tenderness with words and gesture every day.

→ Give importance to the psychical-spiritual growth of both.

→ Give deepness to your own life as well to the relationship.

→ Be cautious with the destructive forces of your unconscious.

→ Integrate drive (desire); give importance and talk about it.

→ Respect physical needs (health) and take care of them.

→ Experience life time as valuable and use it intelligently.

→ Protect and promote the values of being and living together.

→ Adapt a lot of knowledge to create life with skills.

→ Transform rigid principles (norms) in open patterns for life.

→ Strengthen decisiveness against what could destroy love.

What a shame: Most relationships and marriages live love on a level of 1%.

 Either you learn to love your partner every day and without reserve, or your relationship will fail! There is no paradise for people that live a relationship without the full power of love! You decide!

35. Prepare Yourself for a Relationship

👍 You must prepare yourself for a relationship.

👍 You are responsible for yourself when starting a relationship.

👍 Not being prepared and not learning ends very painfully.

👍 Don't start a relationship if you don't want to learn.

Learn considering some practical facts:

- Mutual interest in the daily reality is important.
- Accept conflicts, tensions, and difficult experiences.
- Respect the differences (character, gender, self-expression).
- Both are mutual and equal of rank.
- Alternate closeness and distance in living together.
- See the biography of both as a part of the self-identity.
- Respect the limits of the partner and the partner's world.
- See daily life as a space of conscious communication.
- Permanent animation and formation of love is essential.
- Daily discussion of all common matters is a must.
- Do not mutually balance your errors (mistakes).
- Respect self-realization as a dedication to one self.
- Reason and intelligence are supporting functions.
- Eroticism and falling in love have their place in daily life.
- Both must develop a high level of self-management.

- Mutual acceptance and satisfaction of sexual lust is indispensable.
- You cannot possess each other in the wholeness of being.
- Seduction and lust as animating forces are part of love.
- Both need capacity and effort for understanding.
- Self-identity of both changes every few years.
- Balance living together with female and male qualities.
- Find common solutions to objective questions / matters.
- Find orientation together in dreams, intuition and meditation.
- Discuss and accept distribution of roles.

Primitiveness: Most people are absolutely not prepared when they start a relationship, even unable to constructively live a relationship.

 Either you prepare yourself for a relationship, or your relationship will end in huge amounts of problems and conflicts! There is no paradise for people that live a relationship without preparing themselves for it! You decide!

36. Satisfy your Desire for Sex and Tenderness

👍 *Making love is a human encounter.*

👍 *Sex gives strength, hope and new life forces.*

👍 *Good sex makes positive, peaceful, and happy.*

👍 *Sex strengthens self-esteem and self-confidence.*

👍 *Sexual encounter is a wonderful human gift.*

The soul needs to give and receive a lot of signs of love:

→ Give a little kiss, a tender caress, a loving word, often a little gift.

→ Give emotional words of attention even in unimportant moments.

→ Appreciate the other's presence with a smile.

→ Show interest in all that the partner may think, feel, and wish for.

→ Give a small support even if it is not necessary.

→ Spoil your partner with all kinds of giving.

→ Express respect, understanding, and cooperation.

→ Satisfy your partner's need and desires as much s possible.

→ Create small events for new experiences.

→ And if you are alone, masturbate as much as you feel well with.

→ With occasional sex you must always protect yourself.

Making love also means learning about the partner's individuality and expressions, learning about what each one likes and dislikes.

People that say sexual satisfaction is unimportant or "dirty" are stupid, neurotic, perverse, false, liars, power-obsessed, driven by religious lunacy; they hate and reject human life.

- Sexual experiences with love produce joy.
- Sex and sexual pleasure have a lot to do with love.
- Sexuality is always a self-expression of a person.
- Living sexuality reflects the whole human being.
- Expressing tenderness always also includes a message.
- Intimate tenderness aims to give pleasure with: "I love you".
- Every sensual experience reaches the whole person.

 Either you satisfy your sexual desire, or you become rigid, stubborn, despotic, bossy, frigid, and very annoying! There is no paradise for people that do not live their sexual drive! You decide!

37. Become Aware of your Sexual Attitudes

👍 *Your sexual attitudes, your sexual drive and behavior are the result of your education and life experiences.*

👍 *Become aware of your sexual attitudes, your sexual drive and behavior, and revise inefficient components.*

Reflect your experiences, attitudes, and sexual behavior:

→ Understand which partner mainly influenced your life.

→ Reflect what you learned from your previous partner(s).

→ Contemplate your embarrassing experiences.

→ Become aware of how you see men and women.

→ Remember how you have been enlightened on sexual matters.

→ Think about what you liked most about your partner(s).

→ Remember what hurt you especially about sexual experiences.

→ Think about the importance of fidelity and supporting each other.

→ Find out what you like about the masculine / feminine body.

→ Identify the attitudes, norms and prohibitions you experienced.

→ Identify sexual prejudices you have about men / women.

→ Remember the most embarrassing sexual experiences you

had.

You must reflect yourself in order to have satisfying sex:

- You are rude, not tender, mostly in a rush to copulate (to end).
- You reject your body and your desire to make love.
- You have little ability to show feelings and speak about them.
- You can't talk about sexual wishes, fantasies, and desires.
- You have had a religious education that rejects sexual lust.
- You have experienced sexual traumas (abuse).
- You are scared of exploring your body and sexual drive.
- You, being a mother / a father, have lost your interest in sex.
- Your biography is overcharged with conflicts and problems.
- You don't trust your partner; you even fear your partner.

The misery: There is no satisfying sexual life in the world of politicians and other leaders, and especially not in the catholic community.

 Either you reflect yourself, your attitudes and sexual experiences, or you block the development of love with mutual satisfaction! There is no paradise for people that block sexual satisfaction! You decide!

38. Live a Constructive Relationship

☝ Be realistic about living a constructive relationship.

☝ Living a relationship means lifelong permanent learning.

☝ Learning with and from the partner promotes fulfillment.

☝ To get success in living together with a partner of the other gender you need good communication skills, appropriate rules, and an all-round balanced life management.

Communication rules

→ Do not humiliate, hurt, depreciate, and don't mock.

→ Do not interpose, exaggerate, and don't lose the tone.

→ Discuss matters cooperatively and complementarily.

→ Communicate clearly, objectively, and directly.

→ Listen, understand, select, and let the partner articulate.

→ Adequately express problems, wishes, questions, feelings.

→ Hold and sometimes allow distance and autonomy.

→ Respect the partner as an autonomous person.

→ Consider spiritual ties (e.g. dreams), intuition, and meditation.

→ Consider the physical state of yourself and of your partner.

→ Understand the past as a challenge for learning.

→ Continuously think and renew values, norms and attitudes.

Do not live together with a partner if you don't want to learn these communication rules and the all-round life management together! Most people have an absolute primitive understanding of a relationship with love!

All-round balanced relationship management:

- Live and mutually promote Individuation.
- Learn and practice an efficient self-management.
- Regularly create common experiences that bring joy.
- Form a couple-identity through the common biography.

 Either you learn to live a constructive relationship, or you will fail with the relationship and especially with yourself and your life! There is no paradise for people that do not live a constructive relationship with love! You decide!

39. Make the Right Marriage Promises

👍 *Marriage is of highest archetypal value.*

👍 *Marriage means the unification between man and woman.*

👍 *Marriage is a concept to grow with and through the other gender to become psychologically and spiritually a whole, to achieve completeness.*

You are ready to get married if you are able to promise the following to your beloved partner: "I promise...:

➔ to understand you in your verbal and non-verbal expressions,

➔ to support you and not to not abuse your weaknesses,

➔ to find compromises and to encourage and assist you

➔ to constructively deal with disagreements and arguments,

➔ to satisfy your needs and desires in a way you feel well with,

➔ to balance my interests with your interests,

➔ to respect your feelings and emotional limits,

➔ to clarify misinterpretation and misunderstanding,

➔ to care for you and your being (mind, soul, heart, desires, health),

➔ to promote your psychological and spiritual development,

→ to respect the rules of partnership,

→ to communicate constructively,

→ to understand your dreams and thoughts and opinions,

→ to objectively discuss based on correct information,

→ to always give you the utmost attention,

→ to give you opportunities to realize your talents, self-expressions,

→ to elaborate important decisions with you in a democratic way,

→ to never blackmail or force you against your soul,

→ to respect all your qualities as a complementary part of me,

→ to stay with you in good and bad times,

→ to give highest priority to our love and to take care of this love.

Don't get married and never procreate a baby if you are not ready to make these marriage promises!

People get married and then they don't know what they have done.

 Either you learn to give the right and necessary marriage promises, or you play with yourself and your partner! There is no paradise for people that play with love promises! You decide!

40. Praise the Bond of Marriage

☝ *The Archetype "marriage" has got nothing to do with a homosexual relationship ("marriage").*

☝ *Using the term "marriage" for a homosexual union is like child-abuse, and it is a spiritual crime against the Archetypes "marriage" and "family"!*

■ A marriage is not simply a living-community. Marriage is not a mere realization of love; the meaning includes more than a human and legal space to procreate and educate children.

■ Understand the essential meaning of marriage and learn everything that is necessary and useful to get life long success. Marriage needs to be protected and developed in all its capacities by both partners. Creating partnership-like an interesting life strengthens marriage.

■ The core meaning of the term "marriage" is: Going through the process of psychical-spiritual growth as man and woman to achieve the balanced union of the masculine and feminine archetypes, and in the mutual participation of this process.

■ "Marriage" has a strong psychical-spiritual focus; and the meaning is "unimpeachable". Only through the aspect of "marriage" as a ritual celebration does it have its legitimacy.

■ The homosexual "marriage" has got nothing in common with that meaning; the term "marriage" is not justified with any argument and as an archetypal meaning absolutely not legitimate; it's nonsense!

■ There are definite psychoanalytical explanations for homosexuals that unconscious drive conflicts are caused by experiences in their relationship with mother and father.

■ The consequences are: they disgrace the archetype of marriage and the genuine family values by abusing this term for their homosexual relationship with their neurotic conflict. Their demand is like a dogma. This desecration of the "marriage"-Archetype can never be accepted! A disgusting shame!

 Either you learn to respect and protect the Archetypes of marriage and family, or you commit a spiritual crime against the eternal holy values! There is no paradise for people that abuse the highest Archetypes of the Soul! You decide!

41. Resolve your Relationship Conflicts

👍 *There is no love or relationship life without arguments, quarrels, crises, problems and conflicts.*

👍 *Conflicts in a relationship are often also a conflict with oneself.*

👍 *If you want to understand your partner and relationship, you must first understand yourself.*

👍 *If you don't see your own psychical life, you can't see the psychical life of your partner.*

👍 *One's own self-relation is reflected in all relationship conflicts.*

Search for the causes of your love and relationship conflicts:

→ Love conflicts are often caused by the unconscious inner life.

→ Ideals, fears, norms and much more are sources of conflicts.

→ Deficits experienced in the childhood long to be satisfied later on in life.

→ Unrealistic ideas about the inner life and relationship life.

→ The "bad" ("evil") in the other is one's own unseen "bad" aspect.

→ Super values (ideals) of perfectionism destroy a relationship.

→ Nagging about meals, behavior (etc.) produces problems.

→ The inability to deal with tensions and conflicts causes more conflicts.

→ Not communicating leads to a cul-de-sac without a way out.

→ Self-lies lead to a huge amount of life lies and artificialities.

Willingness, readiness, and ability to work out any and every issue and difficulty that will come up, expressed as a mutual life long commitment, is much more important than a "high match" in interest, hobbies, tastes, and all the wonderful feelings of being in love.

95% of people simply ignore their problems and conflicts. But you are responsible to solve crises, problems and conflicts!

 Either you learn to resolve problems, conflicts and crises, or the burden you carry will become bigger and bigger until the "explosion"! There is no paradise for irresponsible people that are too lazy to learn how to resolve love conflicts! You decide!

42. Manage your Family Efficiently

👍 *The most essential core of family management is LOVE!*

👍 *Only with knowledge and skills can a family life succeed.*

👍 *In the management of a family, love creates a bond.*

You must become aware of the immense value of a family:

➜ Family management is based on the human longing for having a partner, growing together with the partner and the children.

➜ Living together always includes giving appreciation, showing affection, loving and encouraging each other.

➜ Love accepts the differences in each person during the entire life course where all members are growing.

➜ A positive life philosophy, spiritual and general human values, as well as faith, hold the family together.

➜ Positive feedback, encouragement, and signs of affection create the family "spirit" on a daily basis.

➜ Family life has to be organized: each member has his "place" and all members have to contribute for a living together that works well.

➜ A family needs time to relax together, to have fun together, and to experience the world together (e.g. holidays, leisure).

→ A well working family regularly makes time for talking and listening, sharing daily chores and taking decisions together.

→ Family time also creates a sense of belonging where all members can share ideas, thoughts, and experiences.

Nowadays a family is exposed to countless influences: media, internet, advertising, countless goods, thousands of toys, electronic games, mobile phones, countless consumer goods, cars, accessories, constantly changing fashion products, etc. The mega-supermarket has destroyed all parental efforts for a good education of their children. Even small children are already brainwashed and manipulated to want unlimited fun.

Family values are in danger! Learn a lot about family life!

 Either you learn to live an efficient family management and to respect the high values of a family, or you destroy one of the highest Archetypes of the Soul! There is no paradise for irresponsible people that disrespect and destroy family values! You decide!

43. Educate your Children Appropriately

👍 *To correctly educate a child is a demanding responsibility.*

👍 *The ability to educate children demands knowledge and skills.*

Some orientations and rules for educating children:

→ Give the children self-esteem, affection, emotional support.

→ Encourage your children and transmit understanding.

→ Children must learn the importance of routines and rituals.

→ A way of educating children is by talking and listening.

→ Talking resolves most critical situations in the family life.

→ Obviously, listening is equally part of talking.

→ Putting down, threatening and blaming makes a child feel bad.

→ Criticizing with the right words and attitudes can create improvements.

→ Punishments form part of education; but it must be adequate.

→ Children must get the chances to learn by doing.

→ A never-ending fight for control doesn't make a situation better.

→ Routines are a way of educating a child about ways of living.

→ Children must learn how to use money, a mobile phone, the internet...

→ Educate your children through the way you live and behave.

Children copy what they see in their parents, on the television, on the street, in magazines, in other families, and in friends. Children want to explore the world. They must learn how damaging it can become not to choose value-oriented. Strong discipline, efficient working and learning attitudes, together with an understandable and comprehensive explanation, must form part of the children's education.

Always respect genuine inner needs, live love with intelligence and Spirit. This is the best possible foundation of educating your children. But your child will always have the free choice to follow your vivid model, to correct and to improve it, or to reject it.

 Either you learn to educate your children by living yourself in permanent learning, or you destroy the soul of your children! There is no paradise for irresponsible parents that are not a good role model and do not promote psychical-spiritual development! You decide!

44. Decide Carefully about Abortion

👍 *It is your absolute duty to thoroughly think with your partner if you want to procreate a baby.*

👍 *It is also your duty to take appropriate measures so that you do not create an undesired baby.*

👍 *It is definitely not advisable to procreate a baby if you are not educated for this responsibility.*

If you decide about abortion, you must consider some facts:

→ A woman, having aborted without elaborating this event thoroughly, will even in the far future feel tears of pain and guilt.

→ The event of an abortion and a repressed guilt always creates a new destiny, has a strong impact in future developments.

→ Regressions into the prenatal times show us that with the procreation a soul is bonded to this biological being.

→ The soul of a fetus has a paranormal consciousness and perception, and a corresponding emotional experiencing.

→ Men also unconsciously feel a certain responsibility for the new life. Repressing responsibility forms a rigid character.

→ Men too can be pursued during decades from the nagging question: "What kind of daughter or son would it be today?"

→ The decision for abortion is a very difficult challenge. In all cases professional advice and support is appropriate.

→ Once aborted, the decision cannot be revoked. The procreated baby and rejecting to accept it, forms a person.

→ There are very difficult human and economic circumstances that make it appropriate or necessary to abort.

→ The enormous consequences of such a moral and human decision should at least lead to responsible attitudes in one's own sexual life, fully considering such a risk.

Never forget: With procreation, a soul is immediately connected with the fetus. This soul is fully aware of this fact.

 Either you are fully responsible for the consequences of an appropriate abortion and learn for the future, or guilt will dominate your unconscious life! There is no paradise for women and men who are irresponsible in the matter of an abortion! You decide!

45. Reduce Stupid Arguments

👆 *With self-education you become free from destructive and inefficient coding that arises from the childhood, the parents, and from previous life experiences.*

👆 *Become aware of learnt patterns such as imitating mother or father, repeating parental patterns of quarrels, or ways of communicating.*

Some constructive practical suggestions:
→ Express your needs, also for leisure clearly and concretely.

→ Communicate so that your partner can understand you.

→ Do not ignore something in order to avoid arguments.

→ Take your feelings and those of your partner seriously.

→ Don't show preoccupation in order to avoid listening.

→ Don't play around in order to give low attention.

→ Start an important communication at an appropriate time.

→ Don't make a habit out of eating, drinking, watching TV due to frustration.

→ Admit to be deeply preoccupied with yourself and explain yourself.

→ Don't behave aggressively in order to suppress something.

→ Don't behave affectedly, playing the offended or annoyed person.

→ Don't be unpunctual as a hidden way of manipulating.

➜ Don't make a mess as a form of a protest.

➜ Discuss and solve problems with disagreements.

Find new views and new attitudes:

- Talking to each other is a learning process; contemplate about it.

- Every partnership is sometimes faced with strong arguments.

- Some quarrels may cover deeper emotions about love and trust.

- To have a strong confrontation with the partner can happen.

- A humiliating criticism at work often affects the life at home.

- Good friends can produce more problems in a difficult situation.

- Dogmas are poison for a partnership with Individuation.

- Think about this: "Do I really want to destroy my relationship?"

Most relationships are completely contaminated with lies and cheat.

 Either you learn how to reduce stupid arguments, or you will have more and more arguments! There is no paradise if you don't pursue the right way of dealing with arguments! You decide!

46. You Decide about Divorce (or Separation)

👍 *In 7 of 10 critical situations with divorce risk, a solution is possible.*

👍 *In most cases underlying conflicts in relationships can be solved.*

👍 *It is better to solve relationship matters than to run away from problems.*

There are many reasons that can lead to divorce:

- Being unable to solve one's own problems.
- Unable to quarrel or argue constructively.
- Having married out of a fear to be alone and lonely.
- Conflict with the mutual role expectations: to provide and protect.
- Unable to listen and to articulate (communication abilities).
- Lack of self-love and with that an inability to love the partner.
- An illusion such as thinking that marriage works by itself.
- Inability to genuinely realize oneself (self-realization).
- Victim and actor of life lies and with that of illusions of the zeitgeist.
- Power and revenge games, rejection and hide-and-seek games.
- Unable to show feelings; and to constructively deal with them.

- Infidelity as a result of a stagnating and superficial relationship life.
- Personal life crisis that the person does not want to master.
- Difficult in development of a neurotic character of one or from both.
- Unable to live sexuality and to deal with the problems about it.

The first basic rule: each partner has to face his own being. Dreams tell each one what he has to do and how he can progress.

The second basic rule: Love demands the psychical-spiritual development. If one partner entirely refuses this, divorce is on the table for discussion.

The third basic rule: One has to learn how to love, so that the other partner can be convinced with facts about learning and growing.

If one partner disrespects these rules, divorce is appropriate. Not to divorce can paralyze the entire life and block any fulfillment.

 Either you learn about the relationship difficulties and become responsible for your decision, or you will have even bigger problems in the future! There is no paradise if you deal with divorce in an indifferent way! You decide!

47. Succeed in Choosing the Right Partner

👍 *Explore if your possible partner is ready to learn.*

👍 *Find out if your possible partner is already all-sided formed or in a consciously managed forming process?*

👍 *Discover if your partner is willing to cooperate in managing life?*

Principles:

You and your possible partner must be willing to learn about human beings, about the inner life, about life, love, relationship, dealing with money, education of children, managing family life, interests, etc.

Some attitudes are essential and indispensable to succeed: honesty, trust, faithfulness, understanding, cooperation, a satisfying sexuality, and a fair and open way of communication about everything.

Contemplate carefully:

→ Choose a really good person to live with.

→ You decide with whom you begin a relationship.

→ Don't have unrealistic expectations; it leads to conflicts.

- → If you want a person as your partner, do a lot to love him/her.
- → The inner being of the chosen person is the source of life.
- → Good learning attitudes are required to succeed in love.
- → Don't choose a partner simply because of excited feelings.
- → Aiming for marriage is about sharing the existence on earth.
- → Consider that you and your partner will grow as a person.
- → You will have to face many challenges during your life together.
- → Biographical burdens will produce heavy relationship problems.
- → Don't jump into unknown water because it feels great!

The chosen partner will determine the frame of your life and your psychical-spiritual development for the rest of your life. It makes sense to chose the right partner if you don't want it to become a living nightmare.

 Either you are very cautious in choosing the right partner, or you will have to live with all the uncomfortable consequences! There is no paradise if you start a relationship blindly! You decide!

48. Deal with your Feelings

👍 *Feelings are very important in life.*

👍 *You can understand your feelings.*

👍 *You must form and manage your feelings!*

Manage your feelings with efficient approaches:

→ You want to understand your feelings:
  This is possible with reflection and meditation.
→ You want to be able to deal with your feelings:
  First you have to understand them.
→ You want to be free from inner disruption:
  Understand that which disrupts you from the inside.
→ You want to have positive feelings towards life:
  Make a move towards the real life.
→ You feel an inner burden:
  Search for that heavy burden from inside and solve it.
→ You feel sadness and depressed inside:
  There is something inside that is depressing you.
→ Your state is stressful, moody, and nervous:
  Analyze exactly what pushes you to this state.
→ You lack true hope and confidence:
  Build it up within you and with real performance.
→ You are unsatisfied with yourself:
  Do what is necessary to find satisfaction.

→ You don't feel "complete":

Find your fulfillment with psychical-spiritual development.

→ You are unhappy:

One can only become really happy with love and Spirit.

→ You feel a lack of inner peace:

Make peace with yourself in your mind and your life.

→ You feel a diffuse guilt:

The biggest guilt is to refuse oneself.

→ You think everything is meaningless:

The meaning of life is to find, form and live one's Self.

 Either you understand, manage and form your feelings, or you will be a victim of your feelings! There is no paradise if you blindly let your feelings take over! You decide!

49. Manage your Energetic State

👍 *Care for the state of your energy.*

👍 *There are many ways to strengthen your energy:*

→ You are feeling tense. Free yourself from stress factors.

→ You feel disharmony inside. Create a balance.

→ You feel inner pressure. Take away the real pressure.

→ You are easily angered. Things have to go the way you like.

→ You are depressed. There are factors pressing your soul.

→ You feel corseted. Norms, attitudes, beliefs corset you.

→ You are unsettled. You don't have inner foothold.

→ You feel insecure. There is a lack of abilities.

→ Your inner life is rigid and armored. The suppression is total.

→ You can react very rigidly. You are not well formed.

→ You only have little life energy. The unconscious eats energy.

→ You don't have a zest for life. Something paralyzes you.

→ You often react with a bad mood. You have no structure.

→ You can be inexplicably destructive. You have inner conflicts.

→ You are infected by moods of others. You are not well

structured.

Use methods to strengthen the state of your energy:
- Create positive images in your mind; balance inner images.
- Focus on efficient thoughts; dissolve inefficient thoughts.
- Accept life, dissolve opposites; reconcile with life.
- Resolve conflicts; form constructive and efficient attitudes.
- Focus on positive meaning; give positive care for the body.
- Meditate, practice mental training; reduce external stimuli.

The global monkey theatre is disgraceful: People spend money without thinking, talk without thinking, judge without thinking, make love without thinking, get married without thinking, speculate without thinking, use their time without thinking, manage their life without thinking, procreate babies without thinking, do business without thinking, believe in whatever without thinking, obey without thinking, and waste their life energy without thinking. Unbelievable!

 Either you strengthen your life energy, or you become destructive and paralyzed with uncontrolled energy! There is no paradise if you do not control and manage your life energy! You decide!

50. Deal with Stress Constructively

👍 A healthy behavior, as prevention and mastering of stress, has to be developed and practiced also through a holistic understanding of human beings.

👍 A healthy behavior is indeed simply a healthy life style that considers the permanent and largely oriented education of human beings.

👍 We should give a life-philosophical foundation to the individual life style with values and attitudes which accept life in its biological and psychical-spiritual entirety.

➔ Stress is an unspecific physical reaction.

➔ Stress isn't just nervous tension.

➔ Stress isn't always the unspecific result of harm.

➔ Stress isn't something which principally must be avoided.

➔ Stress is also (sometimes) the spice of life.

Identify the causes of stress:

💣 noise   💣 driving   💣 money problems

💣 traffic   💣 emission   💣 frustration

- advertising
- bad air
- worry
- conflict, quarrel
- doing nothing
- lack of movement
- push for success
- haste, speed
- people
- challenges
- prestige thinking
- wrong nutrition
- violence
- ambitions
- religious norms
- work at the PC
- wrong authority
- diffuse anxiety
- moral attitudes
- distrust
- narrow places
- swindle
- new technologies
- artificial holiday
- lying, lies
- rigid norms
- critical living conditions
- sorrow
- falseness

The capitalistic perversion achieved its peak: The more stress, the better the ego feels, the better the chances for a career; the better one can avoid to love and to live with the inner Spirit.

 Either you deal with stress factors, or you become a victim of stress which hinders peace and happiness! There is no paradise if you ignore the essential stress factors! You decide!

51. Take Care of your Health

👍 *Health is much more than a positive physical state.*

👍 *There are efficient measures for a healthy life style.*

→ Be aware of the sensual feelings that you have.

→ Stand up for your opinions and interests.

→ Speak about anger, rage and temper.

→ Accept strong and also unsettled feelings.

→ Explore new and uncommon ideas.

→ Learn to like being alone sometimes and occupy yourself.

→ Spoil yourself every now and then.

→ Don't feel forced to always solve every problem immediately.

→ Learn to live well, also if things don't go well.

→ Occasionally walk (instead of taking the lift or the car).

→ Often go out into the fresh air.

→ Regularly let fresh air into your home.

→ Avoid noise and bad air, if possible.

→ Switch off the television if the program bores you.

→ Ensure that you have a regular life pattern.

→ Be moderate with cigarettes, alcohol, coffee, sweets, eating.

→ Enjoy eating with time and calmness.

→ Often enjoy your work (minimum 20% of your daily tasks).

→ Manage time pressure without 'swerving'.

→ See sense in your work as well as in your leisure.

→ When driving, respect others, and drive sensibly.

→ Take interest in the biographies of others.

→ Often visit cultural, social and political events.

→ If necessary put your interests on the table with force.

→ Give high importance to the basic values of human beings.

→ Accept inner and external suffering in life.

→ Accept difficult life phases from your past.

The list of possible illnesses, disease, and mental problems is very long. You will most probably run away from this list because you deny and ignore your inner and external life.

 Either you take care of your health, or you risk unnecessary (self-made) health problems! There is no paradise if you ignore and do not take care of your health! You decide!

52. Resolve Problems and Conflicts

☝ *You are responsible to solve your problems and conflicts.*

☝ *You are responsible to learn how to solve problems and conflicts.*

☝ *Solve your conflicts and problems with intelligence and creativity.*

→ Take time to understand the problem before you start solving it

→ Keep all facts clear in your mind

→ Identify the facts which are especially important

→ Prepare a list of questions to deal with the problem

→ Try to be consciously original and to find new ideas

→ It isn't ridiculous if you say anything uncommon or wrong

→ Get rid of cultural taboos which could undermine a solution

→ Draw a diagram so you can visualize the problem

→ Imagine how you will solve the problem

→ Go through the real elements of the problem

→ Divide the problem into parts: solve a part and continue like that

→ Use similar situations, examine the possibility for transfer

→ Keep your mind open and examine the presumption

→ Use different strategies: verbal, visual, calculating, action

→ If you are stuck in an attempt, try another way to go ahead

→ Be watchful of strange situations. You could be near a solution

→ Search for connections between different facts

→ Trust your intuition. Approach a way and see where it leads to

→ Try to guess the way for a solution until it goes ahead

→ To create a big fuss may delay, but can finally lead to the goal

→ Jump over common things, try to invent new methods

→ Try to be objective; evaluate your ideas as if they were alien

Nobody is interested if you solve your problems (conflicts) – or not!

 Either you resolve problems and conflicts, or these conflicts and problems will dominate you; and they will grow and make life very complicated! There is no paradise if you do not resolve your problems and conflicts! You decide!

53. Use a Strategy to Solve Problems

👍 *Creativity is decisive for a strategy.*

👍 *Motivation is essential to apply a strategy.*

👍 *Mental fitness is a precondition to deal with strategies.*

Mastering problems and difficulties requires a plan and a strategy. That means: a systematic, open and transparent planning of possible solutions. Few people do this in their daily life. The effects are evident: bad solutions, no solutions at all, endless trials without any success and a tormenting increase in more and more problems.

1st Step: Analyzing and classifying the problem. What is the problem? How did it come about? How important is the problem? What is part of the problem? Which institution is involved? Who is involved? What is my ideal? Which possibilities are given?

2nd Step: Identifying the deficit of information, life-knowledge, theories, and ideas. What exactly is lacking? Which connections do I not understand? Structure ideas and facts, then define the problem in a new way.

3rd Step: Constructing theories and procuring the necessary information. Search for connections and explanations (causes-effects; networking). Construct a diagram (draw, course-diagram, mind-mapping, etc.). Managing a problem is always also a learning process for all people involved.

4th Step: Draft a possible solution on the basis of theories (X is because of Y). Examine if a solution is feasible. Define the standards of the solution. Prepare the decisions. Analyze the concomitant phenomenon and effects.

5th Step: Realizing the plan of a solution. Action!

6th Step: Evaluation and examination of the success.

Do you want to solve the problem, or do you prefer to live with it for the next few years, until one day it disappears – or perhaps until it increases dramatically? You are responsible for your success!

 Either you work with a strategy to get solutions and a good result, or you try endlessly, with too much effort, a lot of wasted time and little success! There is no paradise if you do not strategically resolve your problems and conflicts! You decide!

54. Overcome Difficult Situations

👍 *You can overcome difficult situations.*

👍 *You can find back to a good life and find happiness.*

Many people experience a hard blow from destiny: a beloved person dies or gets paralyzed, caused by an accident; early death of the parents; or one's own child dies; separation or divorce; unexpected unemployment; bankruptcy because of manifold causes; cancer or an illness with serious consequences; a storm destroys homes and businesses; drought or flood destroy existences; victim of robbery or murder or rape; child abuse; victim of all kinds of violence; loss of saved money through amoral activities of banks; victim of terrorism or war incidents; falling into poverty; and much more...

If you already have had a hard blow from destiny, now, during your whole life you can lament, whine, rage, give up, become an alcoholic, swear vengeance, fall into deep depression; and as a broken person continue living in some way. For a certain time such a reaction is understandable.
To spend the rest of your life as a broken person is never

necessary! Mourn for a certain time. But then: STOP! And act:

→ Reconcile with life over what happened to you!

→ Find back to the high values that you can live on this earth!

→ Elaborate everything that is related to the past event!

→ Start finding yourself again! Discover your inner life!

→ Determine new life aims that are oriented towards inside!

→ Search inside for the Archetypes of the Soul for growing!

→ Bid farewell to the past in very small steps!

→ Organize yourself with furniture, clothes, and everything!

→ Learn a lot about the humans and become a wise person!

→ Go your path, given by your inner life, guided by the Spirit!

→ Fight hard, every day and this for years in order to succeed!

→ Keep a journal; find orientation in dreams and meditations!

→ Your values lie in your inner being: search and live them!

→ You are allowed to find back to joy of life and happiness!

 Either you overcome difficult situations, or these will dominate you for the rest of your life! This would be a complete waste of life! There is no paradise if you do not overcome difficult situations with complete effort! You decide!

55. Master your Psychical Suffering

👍 *You can overcome your psychical suffering.*

👍 *You can find a completely healthy and strong inner life.*

The most widespread psychical sufferings are: Depression, fear, phobias, compulsions, psycho-somatic disturbances and psychical suffering, sleep disorder, headache, migraine, diffuse corporal pains, many forms of allergy, etc.

In a psychical suffering we can discover a variety of aspects: unelaborated experiences, lack of meaning, suppressed rage, self-rejection, disappointments, frustration, repressed sexuality, depressiveness, sadness, passivity, isolation, feelings of deficiency, paralyzed will, feelings of dependency, feelings of inability, minimal self-respect, little assertiveness...

In a certain sense all these people are "healthy", but they suffer from a state that all around is not good. The person who doesn't suffer from the absurdity of the zeitgeist, the delusion of consumption, the greed and unscrupulousness, the barbarity of the state of humanity and the earth, is really ill!

People want to fight against their inner suffering with medicine! That is really very stupid and ignorant! There are much more efficient ways for a definite remedy:

→ Become aware of what depresses you from inside and your life.

→ Elaborate your burden with the right methods.

→ Give yourself self-esteem through activities on a daily basis.

→ Turn towards the hidden dominant forces.

→ Find your self-esteem and your self-confidence.

→ Form ego-strength through self-knowledge and self-education.

→ Concentrate on the important values of your human being.

→ Reconcile your past and your experienced pains.

→ Clarify your repressed problems, difficulties, and conflicts.

→ Find yourself; become entirely yourself with the inner Spirit.

 Either you overcome your psychical suffering, or this situation will increase and dominate you for the rest of your life! This would be a complete waste of life! There is no paradise if you do not overcome your psychical suffering with strong effort! You decide!

56. Live with the Inner Spirit

The "Spirit" is the force that creates our dreams and meditation; and is also the source of intuition and inspiration.

🖐 *The Spirit is an informative, organizing and guiding force.*

🖐 *The Spirit is the wise principle of acting in the soul.*

🖐 *The Spirit is animating, stimulating, and benevolent.*

Characteristics of the inner Spirit:

→ *The Spirit knows for what purpose he transfers messages.*
→ *The Spirit knows the "code program" of the Individuation.*
→ *The Spirit organizes the elaboration of the unconscious mind.*
→ *The Spirit knows the steps to a well balanced being and life.*
→ *The Spirit gives information about God and the transcendence.*
→ *The Spirit identifies solutions where no solution is in evidence.*
→ *The Spirit is the source of religion, of spiritual teaching.*

The Spirit itself faces some outstanding problems:

- The inner Spirit is the highest authority and stands above all religions and dogmatic teaching! But nobody listens to the Spirit.
- The spiritual consciousness of most people is still on an archaic level! Most people avoid getting in touch with their inner Spirit.
- For most people, God (religion, dogmatism) is a substitute for self-knowledge, psychical-spiritual self-education, and the inner Spirit.

Live Spirituality:

- Go the path of the psychical-spiritual process (Individuation)
- Form your own inner (psychical) forces, being responsible for them
- Live love for yourself, a partner, children, others, nature, etc.
- Systematically interpret your dreams and live the conclusions
- Meditate and practice mental-training with all its variations
- Understand the meaning of life in relation to the inner Spirit

 Either you learn to live with spirituality, or you live as a mere human biomass without Spirit! And you can never achieve your fulfillment! There is no paradise if you do not live spirituality with the process of Individuation! You decide!

57. Get the Right Understanding about Dreams

☞ *Everybody dreams at night and mankind has always taken dreams as important.*

☞ *An intelligent force organizes the dream elements to a valuable message.*

☞ *Dreams are the door to the psychical and spiritual universe!*

☞ *The ultimate obligation: Learn to correctly interpret your dreams!*

It is not only an opinion of the people from archaic times, when many people presume, that messages are hidden in dreams. Dream theories are based on the idea, that the messages are useful: they inform, counsel, warn and help to advance in life, especially there where thinking doesn't have any access anymore. That means: an intelligent force organizes the dream elements to a valuable message. This is the "inner Spirit".

Dream interpretation is based on knowledge about the psychical life and the real external life:
The more you know about the psychical life and the life of

human beings in general, the more differentiated your dream interpretation comes out.

The language of dreams is as varied as the variation of language in the real life, in literature, in art and paintings. Seeing this, everyone can notice that this intelligent spiritual force obviously knows much more then the person can know. The inner Spirit can also inform about him-self or about the spiritual world.

Dreams help us in all concerns of life for a good, happy and meaningful life. Dreams show us the path to the deepest inner being, to the essential psychical-spiritual being. Dreams also help us to find orientation in the external reality.

 Either you learn to correctly interpret your dreams and to live the consequences from the dream messages, or you can never find your complete fulfillment and definitely never fulfill the Archetypes of the Soul! There is no paradise without the guidance of the inner Spirit through dreams! You decide!

58. Use the Power of Meditation

🖐 *In meditation, the inner visualization operates the same intelligent force as in dreams.*

🖐 *In order to get success you must meditate with rules to make the inner Spirit work.*

With imagination one can relax, find new forces, prepare a path for the solution to problems, liberate the mind, understand others, find sense to life, elaborate dreams, recognize causes of suffering and difficulties, work through the unconscious, etc. Imagination is a type of meditation, with it we can discover and form the whole psychical and real life to a new form.

Contemplation focuses the archetypes which reflect general structures of the psychical forces, of the processes of transformation of the psychical life, of the essential life themes, of sense (meaning) and values and also of the transcendental reality. General symbols reflect the concrete basic themes of the existence which concern all of us. Contemplation creates the access to the mystery of the human being.

Meditating correctly means:

→ Determine what you want to reach: Knowledge, change, strength.

→ Determine the images and symbols with which you will work.

→ Call the images and proceed the image course well-aimed, controlling passively or actively.

→ Feel the meaning. Interpret the result like a dream.

→ Formulate consequences for your life and evaluate them after having realized the meaning.

→ Always start with a short relaxation exercise.

 Either you learn to correctly meditate, or you can never live from the inner spiritual source; and therefore never find your complete fulfillment and never fulfill the Archetypes of the Soul! There is no paradise without the guidance of the inner Spirit through meditation! You decide!

59. The Reasons why you Must Work for the Paradise

☠ Most big nations around the globe are ready to start WWIII at any time, with a total of more than 7 million soldiers and contractors ready for action.

☠ The economic crisis up to 2010 was only a prelude of what is going to come: the total collapse of the economic systems.

☠ Most oceans and seas are horrifyingly contaminated and destroyed, especially the flow of their natural current.

☠ Food resources, especially fish, rice and wheat, are extremely scarce due to the consequences of the climate change.

☠ The most important global media, especially in all industrialized nations, are in the hands of a few that manipulate humanity.

☠ In the USA and in many EU countries more and more laws are being created which are all copies from the Nazi-époque.

☠ In the past years a few thousand people have taken away

trillions of dollars and Euros from 80% of the population.

☠ The control and punishment of citizens in the USA and in Europe has reached the level previously seen at the time of the Nazis.

☠ The tragedy of 9/11 and global terrorism were fabricated to allow for war, to make harsh laws and to take inhumane measures.

☠ With the new smoking bans politicians want to drastically reduce social encounters that share critical thoughts.

☠ Since years "they" are exploring human made weather, tsunamis, drought, heat waves, and earthquakes in order to start a war.

☠ Everywhere there are laws prohibiting anyone from asking critical scientific questions about historical facts, especially about events from the 20th Century.

☠ 80% of what pupils and students learn (philosophy, social science, psychology, business, history) is irrelevant for life.

☠ More people died and got injured in the past 60 years through car traffic accidents and fine dust pollution than from WWII.

☠ The global car traffic system, including its industry has

destroyed more environment than all wars of the past 300 years combined.

- ☠ 9 out of 10 fathers and mothers educate their children without adequate knowledge, without constructive skills and attitudes.

- ☠ There are approximately 6,000 powerful people that rule the entire Western world; and they want their "new world order".

- ☠ There are megalomaniacs driven by religious psychosis in power that are orchestrating the destruction of any global balance.

- ☠ The CIA, MI5, and Mossad are practically acting beyond any government control and mostly beyond international laws and human values.

- ☠ Christianity and Islam (together 4.5 billion people) have not been able to establish peace on earth and to live the values of love.

- ☠ Christianity and Islam do not educate people for their entire psychical-spiritual development with the inner Spirit.

- ☠ Christianity and Islam have failed to promote, to teach and live the Archetypes of the Soul for fulfillment and highest missions.

☠ In the near future, the catastrophes and damages due to climate change around the globe will cost trillions of dollars every year.

☠ The "pest" that contaminates humanity: greed, megalomania, perversion, psychosis, narcissism, lies, falseness, and sadism.

☠ In the past 600 years the West has committed incredible genocides, stolen wealth, goods and lands all in the name of God.

☠ During 2,000 years Christianity has committed endless dire crimes and wars, oppressed and enslaved many folks, all in the name of J.C.

☠ Every day the sewage and waste of 2-3 billion people goes into the oceans and ground; in 25 years this amount will double.

☠ In 25 years there will be millions of tons of nuclear waste on this earth and nobody knows how to decontaminate or get rid of it.

☠ In 50, 100, 1,000 and even more years people will still have to pay for the maintenance of our nuclear waste from today.

☠ There are more than 100,000 chemical elements contaminating our environment, including the soil, water, air, and some even in our food.

☠ Every year 70 million new cars are produced; in 50 years that will be more than 3,500,000,000. One day the resources will be gone, the planet destroyed.

☠ In 70-90 years the planet will be completely different due to the increase of sea level (30-70 cm) and chaotic weather conditions.

☠ The amount of agricultural land will diminish, the quality of fertile ground will worsen; people will need to eat laboratory prepared food.

☠ Drinking water is becoming more and more scarce; also water for agriculture. The future: dying from famine or thirst, or going to war!

☠ The Western historiography is full of lies, distortions, ignorance, and misinterpretations. The past always determines the future!

☠ History is not reconciled. Conflicts from centuries ago will erupt over and over again. There is no solution beyond the truth.

☠ There are millions of lobbyists luring and blackmailing politicians every day. Lobbyism is epidemic, destroys democracy and transparency.

☠ Governmental accreditations have led to business, economic and political failure, to alienated education and soulless psychology.

☠ "God wrote / said": This is a marketing trick used since thousands of years. It is never God, but always the inner Spirit through dreams.

☠ The miracles of J.C. are a fairy tale or a religious psychosis used as a marketing trick. Miracles do not address the inner life.

☠ The Western governments have trillions ($/€) of debt. Western people live and consume at costs of the next 4-6 generations.

☠ Praying doesn't form a human's inner life, doesn't promote self-knowledge, dream interpretation or the psychical-spiritual process.

☠ 65% of illnesses and accidents are due to the Western style of life, ways of thinking, stupid attitudes, and lack of contemplation.

☠ Politics is a marsh of lies, falseness, games, intrigues, distortion, cheat, narcissism, lunacy, and indifference towards the citizens.

☠ Unemployment worldwide will grow and nobody cares that "working" is a genuine human inner need that today is rotten.

☠ Parents in the USA talk 3 minutes per day to their kids, but watch 6 hours of TV (average); in the EU this sadness is not much better.

☠ Many lies about other countries are orchestrated with the sole aim of going to war for resources and establishing a fascist world order.

☠ J.C. and the "holy" Mary are dehumanized fake ideals, and devaluate each man and woman to a very inferior human being.

☠ "Jesus said:" is a big lie. Nobody knows what he said. 60-80 years after his death some unknown people started writing about him.

☠ The 4 Evangelists didn't exist. Nobody knows who wrote the gospels, changed thousands of times during centuries for brainwashing purposes.

☠ In 40 years 10 billion people will live on this earth. Balance, democracy, safety, health, education, love and peace will be gone.

☠ Babies born today and in the future have to pay for all damages and to suffer from poverty, misery, hunger, contamination, wars.

☠ Even if you are already 40-50 years old, you will have to live a nightmare in 20-40 years, and no pension will be available!

→ Do you want all this for your future, the future of your children, and the following generations? If yes, you will not get into Paradise!

60. Awake Now... Fast!

Regardless of whether you are a "normal" human being from an industrialized, capitalistic, Christian or Jewish folk, or a person in a special position as a politician, teacher, professor, expert, millionaire, billionaire, manager (CEO), priest, Cardinal, Pope, king, etc., with a probability of 80-90% your ancestors and parents, teachers, friends, your religion, the media and your environment have made you what you are today (you can choose what matches with you):

→ An inferior, unreasonable human of minor value

→ An unidentified animal without instinct

→ A blind, brainwashed human biomass

→ A conceited bigmouth without truthfulness

→ A being full of lies, self-lies and life-lies

→ A deformed, distorted, disfigured human being

→ A crushed, chained and suppressed being

→ An artificial, superficial vivid object

→ A very weak, adulterated copied product

→ A greedy, ravenous, insatiable monster

→ A bragger, impostor, bluffer, gambler

→ An uninformed, ignorant, dull, primitive creature

→ A babbler and talker poisoning the environment

→ A naive, gullible and easy seducible sloth

→ An archaic, perverse, psychopathic driven creature

→ An inflated narcissist with a completely disfigured ego

→ A follower, copycat, stereotype of the collective

→ An animalistic being with a completely rotten inner core

→ A hypocritical, pitiable, embarrassing figure of fun

→ A cushy, lazy, indolent, fastidious human biomass

→ A destroyer, breaker, spoiler, embitterer, hater

→ An inutile, only taking and stealing being

→ A very low-thinking, even unable to think pre-hominid

→ A vivid, chaotic, emotional, energetic biomass

→ A highly bred, self-alienated, mad being

→ A lying, false and brutal creature unable to love

→ A boring, bossy person too lazy to learn,

→ An ego-driven, blind "I do what I want"-machine

→ An indifferent, irresponsible, dull inferior human

→ A suppressing, displacing, falsifying, distorting person

→ An obsessed, religious-psychotic driven person

→ An inner weak beast, strengthened only by external things

→ A slave, exploited, abused, misused, violated, raped person

→ An exploiting, enslaving, desecrating, oppressing thief

→ A devil, a beast, a thoroughly evil being

→ A bellicose, a warlike, predacious, killing beast

→ A liar, dispraiser and destroyer of psychical-spiritual values

→ An unreasonable, scrupulous, violent, relentless creature

→ An insane, tricky, inhuman being

→ A lunacy obsessed figure, a global mass killer

→ A destroyer of nature, the species, the climate and the planet

→ A human poisoning trust, hope, love, Spirit, the truth

→ A deicide, a killer of the truth, a destroyer of love and the Spirit

→ A frightening nightmare in the name of J.C.

→ A pest for humanity that shall never have a future

→ An absolute sad and hopeless case for God and the Spirit

→ A desperately futile creature for a Messiah?

Paradise is closed for all these archaic people! They will not get in! I will never allow that Paradise will be poisoned and contaminated by such people!

If you form part of the rare exceptions, then, you are a true (archetypal) copy of the psychical-spiritual human being for the future of humanity. This is hope. But, if you are one of those inferior, very dangerous human biomasses, then today you can learn and change yourself towards a "genuine human".

If you don't want to change, then, you are a danger for humanity and the planet – and your soul is really lost. Because with such an archaic-diabolic state you will in no way come into Paradise. And in your life you do not deserve anything better than WWIII – the result of this strange being.

How can I ever forgive you if you don't want to become a human? I don't want to convince you! It's enough that 10,000 braggers are doing it hypocritically with lies and dirty tricks. I have lost all hope that you want to realize the Archetypes of the Soul. But I have everything, with rock-solid certainty, that can guide the survivors of WWIII to a good future towards the true human being.

This is not racism and not slander. This is a philosophical, historic and psychoanalytical scientifically proven result; certainly shortly comprised with some accentuated terms. My intention is humanity with the Archetypes of the Soul, with peace, truthfulness, hope, love and the inner Spirit.

Made in the USA
Charleston, SC
19 January 2016